A FEW STEPS IN THE RIGHT DIRECTION

GIVE YOURSELF THE CHANCE YOU DESERVE

KENDRICK SAVAGE, PhD

WESTBOW
PRESS®
A DIVISION OF THOMAS NELSON
& ZONDERVAN

Copyright © 2022 Kendrick Savage, PhD.

All rights reserved. No part of this book may be used or reproduced by any means, graphic, electronic, or mechanical, including photocopying, recording, taping or by any information storage retrieval system without the written permission of the author except in the case of brief quotations embodied in critical articles and reviews.

This book is a work of non-fiction. Unless otherwise noted, the author and the publisher make no explicit guarantees as to the accuracy of the information contained in this book and in some cases, names of people and places have been altered to protect their privacy.

WestBow Press books may be ordered through booksellers or by contacting:

WestBow Press
A Division of Thomas Nelson & Zondervan
1663 Liberty Drive
Bloomington, IN 47403
www.westbowpress.com
844-714-3454

Because of the dynamic nature of the Internet, any web addresses or links contained in this book may have changed since publication and may no longer be valid. The views expressed in this work are solely those of the author and do not necessarily reflect the views of the publisher, and the publisher hereby disclaims any responsibility for them.

Any people depicted in stock imagery provided by Getty Images are models, and such images are being used for illustrative purposes only. Certain stock imagery © Getty Images.

Scripture taken from the King James Version of the Bible.

ISBN: 978-1-6642-8472-2 (sc)
ISBN: 978-1-6642-8474-6 (hc)
ISBN: 978-1-6642-8473-9 (e)

Library of Congress Control Number: 2022921612

Print information available on the last page.

WestBow Press rev. date: 12/23/2022

CONTENTS

Dedication vii
Note About the Book ix
Chances xi
Introduction xv

Chapter 1   Savage Words 1
Chapter 2   Can Eye See? 9
Chapter 3   STEPS 21
Chapter 4   What Happened? you Happened! 29
Chapter 5   Shoes with Souls 37
Chapter 6   More than a Shell 45
Chapter 7   The Red Carpet 53
Chapter 8   The Testimony 59
Chapter 9   Outside Smiling/Inside Hurting 67
Chapter 10 The Goliaths of Life 75
Chapter 11 Waking up with Victory 83

Special Message: S.H.A.P.E 89
Notes 99
Acknowlegements 101

DEDICATION

To my parents, Melvin and Ola Mae Savage, thank you for pouring everything in me that you had. I am who I am because of you. You ran your leg of the race with grace and purpose! I wish you were still here! I promise to continue to carry the torch the best I can!

To my wife, Jamye, your strength is simply amazing! Thank you for standing by my side. Thank you for supporting and loving a man who is always in the clouds! I love you.

To daddy's little girls, Kurrie, Kenley, and Kambry daddy loves you with everything I am. Thank you for all the nail sessions, tickle times, time with dolls, hair sessions (I'll get better) and the extra hugs. Daddy will always be there to lead the way with love, kisses, and support!

NOTE ABOUT THE BOOK

I started writing this book around 2010. I wrote and finished it and then decided to put it on the shelf for a few reasons! First, I started worrying about results (we'll get to that later), and secondly, I doubted what I had to say. None of these points represent a few steps in the right direction. Over the years I've been able to overcome these excuses and what you have before you today is a mixture of where I was then and where I am today! Most importantly, I'm happy to get to a place to take a chance on myself.

Throughout this book you will see me using the phrase **a few steps in the right direction**. This phrase will signify pivotal or very important moments that occurred in my life that ultimately steered me in the right direction. These are moments where I had a choice of going either left or right, backwards or forwards, to listen or not to listen, or to give up or keep going. The phrase also represents inspirational moments, moments of impact, and beneficial people in my life. We all have these moments. Moments that prompt us to make decisions that impact our lives. Some come out of nowhere, whereas others we see coming like headlights on a dark road. Nevertheless, if handled carefully, these moments can serve as **a few steps in the right direction** if we pay attention.

Now, read with me for more inspiration as to why I wrote this book. This book is not me preaching to you or giving you a sermon. I do use biblical scriptures for reference and I talk about my relationship with God because those are my beliefs. This book is about giving yourself a chance at whatever life or dreams you have envisioned for yourself. Every word written in this book is meant to inspire and awaken the greatness within you. I have written these words to cause you to think, to energize you, and to get you moving on your dreams. Personally, I spent years allowing fear to keep some of my ambitions untapped. Sometimes I was simply afraid of what others might say and sometimes I was scared of failing. Jay Shetty, podcast host and author of *Think Like A Monk*, says "The longer we hold on to fears, the more they ferment until eventually they become toxic." So, goodbye to that! And make sure you are not allowing others to have power over a gift where they have no dominion! **A few steps in the right direction!** It's simple. They didn't supply you with your gift, God did that. Again, my belief. Regardless of what and why, you do have a gift! So, don't give them the power to stop your movement. Throughout this book you are going to read quotes from actors, preachers, comedians, entertainers, rappers, and educators to help me to get you to understand the message that is being delivered. Everyone has a story. Anyone can contribute. I hope this book increases your confidence and brings light where there is darkness. I want you to be encouraged and fight for the life that you were meant to live. Be tenacious and never give up, ever! I may never meet you but I pray that this book blesses you mightily and that you will gain strength, courage, and understanding. Life is a journey or as some may say, a marathon, and there are so many steps in life. The steps that you are encouraged to take in this book are meant to move you forward. But you have to be willing to give yourself a chance. On the next page is a spoken word piece that I have written to introduce the feelings that we go through when we fail to take the chances we were meant to take. I hope you enjoy the poem and the rest of this book. Grab my hand and take **a few steps in the right direction!**

CHANCES

What do you do when the road less traveled becomes even less because you are afraid to make a choice, too scared that the invoice will cause you to pay more for choosing, so you think you are better off losing. You see for some people life is about always playing it safe and looking at others peoples' race instead of running in your own lane you would rather get out of your own frame and picture others doing what you have been assigned and twenty years later you'll probably hit rewind just to reminisce about the opportunities you missed because back then when you were young and strong and couldn't wait to move on you actually stood still, all statued up as if your name was liberty which is a complexity being that you were not liberated at all, but that's the past and now is the present so I write these words hoping you'll give yourself a chance.

Here is how to connect with me or offer comments:
Facebook: @Kendrick Savage
Instagram: @real_dr.savage
Youtube Channel: youtube.com/@ksavagemotivation

A FEW STEPS IN THE RIGHT DIRECTION

GIVE YOURSELF THE CHANCE YOU DESERVE

> In the fell clutch of circumstance
> I have not winced nor cried aloud.
> Under the bludgeonings of chance
> My head is bloody, but unbowed.
>
> Beyond this place of wrath and tears
> Looms but the Horror of the shade,
> And yet the menace of the years
> **Finds and shall find me unafraid.**
>
> From "Invictus"
>
> By William Earnest Henley

As you begin this book, I want you to embrace who you are, believe in who you are, and that you are enough! Let your dreams find you **unafraid!** If there is any clear message of this book, then it is this – Just don't give up and be sure to take a chance on yourself!

I love you and thank you for reading this book!

INTRODUCTION

> I'm proud of you. I'm glad God blessed somebody with some education
>
> – Ola Mae Savage, My mother

> Kendrick, I'm proud of you. I sure am
>
> – Melvin Savage, My father

> There's no way I can pay you back, but my plan is to show you that I understand
>
> – Tupac Shakur, Rapper, Actor, Poet

I begin with the very **first few steps in the right direction** that occurred in my life, my mother and father. My mother, Mrs. Ola Mae Savage, and my father, Mr. Melvin Savage, never wore graduation gowns or walked across a stage on graduation day while family and friends applauded them – not even a high school graduation! I learned very early that success for my life was not necessarily tied to the educational or professional titles and jobs that my parents had or did not have. Just like your past doesn't have to determine your future, what you are born into does not have to determine the rest of your life. As a kid when I would meet people that I deemed as really successful I tended to think their parents were doctors, lawyers, teachers, scientist, bankers, and so on. But this is not always the case. I learned this personally when people treated me this way. They would see some of my successes and automatically assumed my parents held this certain job or title. My parents taught me the ingredients that were needed for a bright future. Ingredients such as hard work, perseverance, determination, and having great character – **A few steps in the right direction!**

I watched my dad for over 30 years deliver propane to people in and around the town of Oxford, MS. Summer, fall, winter, and spring I watched him awake early every morning and go without certain things so that his children could have. There were times he got home so late that we would be in bed, and when we awoke he was already gone to work. This was a lot of work. But we still weren't eating filet mignon or riding in a BMW! But don't get me started about the Chevrolet, cornbread, catfish, and pinto beans! **Mmmmmm…a few steps in the right direction!** You see, material things were not the overall objective, character development was always the objective. There is a song by actor and singer Jamie Foxx where he says, "These cars keep me moving, these planes keep me high, a million-dollar home, and I'm barely getting by." Maybe it was the fact that we didn't have much, but my parents really pushed character over material possessions. They wanted us to place importance on the things that could sustain us. **A few steps in the right direction.** My parents never made a fuss over what we didn't have, but if our character was out of line we definitely heard about it. From my dad, I learned to be positive, dedicated, hardworking, and relentless. He was an overcomer in more ways than he would ever realize. The thing I treasured most about my dad was that I never had to wonder if he would be there. He was always there and that alone has inspired me to be as dedicated as possible to whatever I embark upon. My dad taught me how to be dedicated to whatever I set out to do regardless of how the situation looks. My mom was the best mother you could be to three children. As I reflect on my childhood, I am reminded of the attention she gave to us to ensure we were reared properly. Again, character was first, and she did not take it lightly. A quote, often attributed to Saint Francis of Assisi says, "Preach the Gospel at all times. When necessary, use words." What would the younger me say to this? Yooooo!!! That's HOT! **A few steps in the right direction!** I know this was the goal my mother was seeking. It is not what you say, but what you do. All the energy, time, and love she put into her teachings and lessons have been a blessing. Guess what? We still were not perfect and that remains, but we are better for the journey of life. My mom taught us to be respectful to others and to have respect for ourselves. She reared us to understand the importance of appearance and how we presented ourselves. My mom and my Aunt Ruby were like the police of appearance. I can remember times that if my Aunt Ruby was visiting and she saw us and thought we looked wrinkled, she would make us go to our room and iron those clothes! **A few steps in the right direction.** My mom reared us also to enjoy the laughter of life. This is where my love for comedy and natural ability to find the funny comes from. To my parents, thank you for being giving, loving, forgiving, and making extreme sacrifices. You taught me how to overcome, and most of all, keep standing. I have had the opportunity to accomplish most of my dreams because of your sacrifice. It is important to say that the application of what we are taught is not easy. We spend a lifetime getting better at applying what we learn. I cannot tell you how many gifted, talented, young people I have either met or taught that have ruined their opportunities in life by not applying the very knowledge that I knew they possessed. The truth? I understand it! Again, application is hard and none of us will be perfect. **A few steps in the right direction!** It takes a village to keep you on track. It can take your parents, teachers, coaches, granddaddy, grandmother, and friends. Who's in your village? Yes, ultimately the responsibility is yours. However, it helps to have people in your corner checking on you, asking questions, and making sure you are staying on track. I know for a fact that I would have never made it without my village! My village over time has included my parents, my siblings, my pastors, my friends, college mentors, and relatives. Each I have needed at different times. Gospel artist, Marvin Sapp has a song that says,

> Never would have made it
> Never could have made it, without You
> I would have lost it all
> But now I see how You were there for me

A few steps in the right direction! I want you to go out and show your village that you understand! I feel like one of, if not the greatest gift, that you could give to someone who has taught you anything is to show them that you understand. The bible says, **Wisdom is the principal thing; therefore get wisdom: and with all thy getting get understanding.**[1] Live in a certain way that says, "I will exemplify what it is that you always tried to teach me." You will not be perfect at it, but you can do it! I'm thankful that my parents gave me so much to try to exemplify. For that I love them to the highest! Please take **a few steps with me in the right direction.**

Introduction Reflection Questions

- Who do you have in your village?

- What are some key lessons you have learned from your village?

- What are you doing to honor your village? What are you doing to show them that you understand?

SAVAGE WORDS

Your gift, it looks good on you

– Donald Lawrence, Gospel Artist

I am sure you are wondering why the title SAVAGE WORDS? Let me explain. It has nothing to do with my words being SAVAGE! I just have a great appreciation and passion for words. As a young boy I became really intrigued at how poets could take words and intertwine them, slow them down, or speed them up all to create an affective and exciting delivery. It was so moving and inspiring to me! **A few steps in the right direction.** So moving that it inspired me to become a poet! So, the title is personal to parts of my own story. The fact that the title is SAVAGE WORDS is just my way of thanking God for giving me an appreciation for the craft of using words to impact someone's life. This is all about recognizing the gifts that are within you. I am conscious of this anytime I am using teaching, speaking, storytelling, or using spoken word to illuminate an idea or to inspire. So, in that capacity I try to use words wisely. Where does your gift lie? Don't know what your gift is? Think about this – most gifts come inside a box and wrapped in a bow! If you want to know what your gift is, then you got to unwrap it! Meaning, you have to get busy exploring, asking questions, and paying attention to yourself. What do you enjoy? What comes easily to you? What makes you feel alive? What brings you peace? There is an old adage that says, "The richest place in the world is the cemetery." It is the richest place in the world because there are so many untapped and unopened gifts buried there. They are gifts that were never shared and never explored. How about we not add to this? Let's go find that gift! **A few steps in the right direction!**

Have you ever heard a basketball star say he felt as if basketball was his or her way out or a football star say football was his way out? It happens even in areas such as education. Lifelong formal education becomes a person's way out. Now, as I discuss a way out, I do not mean it resulted in fame and glory, though it could happen, that is not always the case. Most will never see the NBA or NFL and many have no desire to obtain the same degrees or levels of education. So, when I mention a way out, I mean if you pay close attention to it you will realize that it becomes a way of helping you to survive – this gift that you've been given! It relaxes you, takes you to another place, a place of inspiration and hope, and it inspires others. This is something that God has blessed you with that you are talented or gifted at and it helps you to overcome. Sounds great right? But there will always be doubters! They are always there to tell us that we're weird or somehow have our head in the clouds. And I know you have heard this one, "I mean I know you want to do that, but I just don't see how it's gone happen." Sometimes people will even go so far as to tell us that this precious gift is the reason why we are socially awkward or the reason we're not popular. Yeah yeah yeah…yada yada yada…it's simple…pay that stuff no mind use your gift and keep it moving! Just because they can't see your vision doesn't mean it's not real! **A few steps in the right direction!** Yes, it's a lifelong journey. There will always be obstacles. I often think about what would have happened if I had never attempted to tap into my gifts.

Writing has served my life in so many ways. It has not only been therapeutic, but a way to help other people. I am naturally quiet, yet studious and analytical. Therefore, when I do have something to say, it's worth something. **A few steps in the right direction.** Now why am I saying this? I say this because of how THEY tried to make me feel. Let me explain. People, and by people I mean peers, often labeled me as this mute or this guy that had no personality at all, but that was not the case. People will often misjudge what they don't understand. What was my personality benefit? I realized, especially during my teenage years, that I could recall people, situations, and scenarios quite well. The reason? I was paying attention. This brings me to another thing I learned during that time. Find the truth and do your best to stand on it. You have to be willing to walk the path of who you are even if other people make fun of you. I heard this quote once, "Truth is the only safe ground to stand upon." **A few steps in the right direction!** I knew who and what I was. So, I didn't let the noise bother me. Now, none of this made me any better than the next person, but I did learn to appreciate myself and others. It may take you a while to understand it, but your personality was made to fit your gifts! So, embrace who you are. **A few steps in the right direction!** Ok, back to why you have to use your gift.

The using of your gift promotes survival! Why is it that a little girl or boy is blessed to be a comedic genius? There is strength and love in receiving the laughs! You never know, that attention that they get could be the only attention they often get. Not only that, but it helps them survive their world. The one you don't see! **A few steps in the right direction!** The gift is there for a reason. Use it! Why is it that the kid who struggles so much inwardly in life was given the gift to write beautifully and expressively? Writing could be his or her way of surviving the surroundings in which they live. Why is it that the beautiful little girl was blessed to have a lovely voice? It just may be her beautiful **little** voice that causes **HUGE** giants and walls of fear to collapse. Even more, her gift could encourage others to step forward in life. Why is it that a young man was blessed with a gift for drawing? It just might be his way of drawing his way out of a turbulent situation. If he can draw it, then he can conceive it! There are many scenarios but in short what I am saying is that we should thank God for our gifts because whether we realize it or not they return to us exactly what we need in order to keep us pushing, to keep us dreaming, to keep us inspiring a world around us, and to keep us above water so that we can continue to walk in God's calling.

So, my friend, let the fear go! Put it behind you and I pray you change the world for the better! Remember, you will never realize this until you get off the bench, put on your helmet and shoulder pads, and run out onto the field of your life to be an active participant! Maybe one day the fans in the stadium just might rise to give you a standing ovation!

Chapter 1 Reflection Questions

- What do you feel is your gift?

- How could you use this gift to help yourself, your family, and others?

- What would be your response to people who try to talk you out of using your gift?

GOING PLACES

I'm a thinker, a thinker of many things
Sometimes of castles, sometimes of kings
My mind is taken to faraway places
The muscles in my face form new faces

Drawn to new heights and great desires
I think of marshmallows and hot campfires
I can either be here or I can be there
I can be in one place or I can be everywhere

My mind is like a river without a destination
It flows and flows making new creations
I am a thinker in mind, heart, and soul
Many Ideas are new, some Ideas are old

Who can stop my mind? Who can control?
Why should it be contained? Its precious as gold
I will continue to think forevermore
Using it to fly and away I will soar

By: Kendrick Savage

CAN EYE SEE?

> Failure is a feeling long before it's an actual result
> - Michelle Obama, Former FLOTUS and Author

I haven't always known what it was I wanted to be, but from a young age I've known what I wanted to do. Let me explain. I have always known I wanted to change as many lives as possible. **A few steps in the right direction.** But naturally, and like so many others I started losing sight of this as I matriculated through high school. I started focusing so much attention on "the be" and not "the do." The world is designed for us to focus so much attention on what we want to be! Not that there is anything wrong with that, but you find so many kids focusing more on an occupation than what it is they want to do at their core. What is it that you want to do?!! Not a title, but the action and the details! **A few steps in the right direction!** I think if you know what it is you want to do, then you can find and match your gift or passions to an occupation that best fits "your do!" Furthermore, there will more than likely be multiple areas or occupations where you can fulfill your "do" at different points of your life. Put some prayer to it and think about it! Either way, it is going to take vision to do or be anything. The bible says, **where there is no vision the people perish**[1]. Let me explain why vision is so important. I have always had a love and appreciation for wildlife. Eagles, for example have tremendous eyesight. These birds have keen eyesight even at distances that most humans would consider very far away. The truth is that's the type of vision we should all aspire to have regarding our lives. I, was once the kid holding the binoculars, looking for treasure so far away, while missing the greatest treasure of all—the treasure that God had placed within me! God can see beauty when we only see dirt. God can see a future when we seem to have lost all belief. The bible reads, **For I know the thoughts that I think toward you, says the LORD, thoughts of peace and not of evil, to give you a future and a hope.**[2] This chapter is on vision because if we are honest our vision precedes our greatest dreams or sometimes our worst nightmares. Sometimes, our vision is not positive, it can create feelings that lead to dissatisfaction – what I call, nightmares! These are not nightmares that you have one night and it's over and they are not nightmares on Elm Street but nightmares on your street and that street is your life. Some of us live these nightmares every single day for years. We begin to think that the only way to live is through these nightmares while never seeing it's our vision that's the problem. Once you begin to realize this, you can confront the problem. **A few steps in the right direction.**

I am thankful every day for what God has blessed me to accomplish in life. However, I've had to really examine my beliefs and vision at every level. Take a trip with me. As a freshmen college student at The University of Mississippi, I compared myself to other students a lot, minimizing our similarities while magnifying our differences! **A few steps in the right direction!** How well prepared they looked, how they must be smarter than me, how I could never speak like them, lead like them. I would imagine that this is a trap for a lot of young people. The vision that I had of myself was in part based on what I felt others had that I didn't have. That was the wrong vision entirely! I was giving people power and determination in my life and they potentially didn't even know I existed. Truth is, I had what I needed all the time. I came to realize one important thing, that I better start paying myself more attention. Now, I don't mean in a selfish sense. I want you to see your own potential, to recognize the worth that you have right alongside everyone else. **A few steps in the right direction!** Recording artist, Mali Music, has a song called Royalty in which he sings:

> "Look at yourself, take your time,
> Baby, you're royalty!
> Lift your head, come back home
> Brother, you're royalty"

Take time to see yourself, be confident, center yourself, you are royalty! If I focused more attention on what I felt like I didn't have, I would never realize the royalty that God has placed within me! **A few steps in the right direction.**

Sometimes we find ourselves struggling with our confidence. We don't recognize that most of us are more similar than different. Some of us become victims of what life throws as us! Life can make you feel as if there will always be only struggle. Then sometimes we are dealing with imposter syndrome, feeling like we have no business being in certain rooms and trying to open doors that others have walked through. Whatever it is that may attempt to attack your confidence, I want you to hold on to the fact that there are so many people that need you! You hear me? YOU.ARE.NEEDED.IN.THIS.WOLRD. **A few steps in the right direction!** For me, I had to realize there was no benefit to living in the shadows. American author Mary Ann Williamson once said, "Our deepest fear is not that we are inadequate. Our deepest fear is that we are powerful beyond measure. It is our light, not our darkness that most frightens us. We ask ourselves, 'Who am I to be brilliant, gorgeous, talented, fabulous?' Actually, who are you not to be? You are a child of God. Your playing small does not serve the world. There is nothing enlightened about shrinking so that other people won't feel insecure around you. We are all meant to shine, as children do. We were born to make manifest the glory of God that is within us. It's not just in some of us; it's in everyone. And as we let our own light shine, we unconsciously give other people permission to do the same. As we are liberated from our own fear, our presence automatically liberates others." **A few steps in the right direction! The bible says it this way, Ye are the light of the world. A city set on a hill cannot be hid.**[3] Both of these references have encouraged me tremendously over the years in terms of having confidence in the vision for my life. So, as I started to gain more confidence and understand I must give myself a chance I slowly started to do just that. Though it would not be easy, I forced myself to do it because I'd never get to where I wanted to be if I didn't. **A few steps in the right direction.** Actor and author, Will Smith once said, "You got to take a shot. You have to live at the edge of your capabilities." Do it, even if fear is standing right beside you!

So, my sophomore year at the University of Mississippi, I became co-head of the recruitment committee for the LSMAMP I.M.A.G.E Program. I started realizing that if I were going to ever do the things I cared so much about, I had to give myself a chance. I had to push myself beyond my comfort zone. It didn't take long before I found myself at a fork in the road. I had two choices. One, I could put all of myself into it and make a difference or short change myself and let fear keep me from expressing what was inside of me. That fork in the road was me realizing that I had to stop being afraid of who I was. More specifically, even though I held the position, I was still struggling with showing my full self, fearing that it wouldn't be accepted or translate. I desperately didn't want my leadership opportunity to be a waste. So, I took that fork and I started destroying every negative thought, all self-pity, and anything standing in my way. **A few steps in the right direction!** Let me just say, I was very intentional. I gave myself some grace by starting small and working my way toward opportunities that would require more out of me. I was done playing it so safe. T.D. Jakes once said, "playing it safe is not always commendable." Sometimes we play it safe only because we are afraid to **step out** and **let out** the great things within us. Back to me pushing myself.

During my junior year at The University of Mississippi, I happened to agree to help the President of I.M.A.G.E give a presentation on a Saturday morning to some high school students. That morning, nervous and jittery I walked into an auditorium filled with high school students to help him give the presentation. I didn't realize how much he was paying attention to me in the present and what he could see in my future. He turns to me on the way out and says, "Ken, I didn't know you had all that in you man! You did really well. I have been watching you." I don't quite remember the rest, but I think he suggested I consider the president role of the organization since he would be graduating that year. His words of confidence in me would change my leadership trajectory forever. It meant a lot to me to hear someone say that. God sent the push I needed! **A few steps in the right direction.**

    I firmly believe the role was meant for me because during the spring I was nominated and actually elected as president, and everything just took off from there. Being president didn't afford me the opportunity to hide! **A few steps in the right direction!** This single moment in my life literally opened the gates of possibility for everything for me. How? The thing I needed to overcome was believing in myself and not being afraid to show others who I was deep inside! Finally, I'd found myself in a position that would act as a catalyst for my life. **A few steps in the right direction!** I could not hide, and I had no choice but to believe in myself. Honestly, I was tired of hiding anyway and the fear of never blooming into my calling was an awful thought to live with. Again, I've always known what I wanted to do. The struggle was believing I could fulfill it and people would be accepting of it. I'm grateful I started realizing it wasn't so much about others, but being who God created me to be. Becoming president was like opening a box of jewels on the inside of me that needed to shine! Again, we must let our light shine, right? During the summer of that year, the I.M.A.G.E Program had a summer bridge component where recently graduated high school minority students who are entering college as STEM majors, take part in, to help bridge the gap between high school and college. Now, at the end of their summer program there is a closing banquet. I still remember it like yesterday, I received a phone call from the project coordinator of the program. She asked me if I would be interested in being the speaker. I was very nervous, but I said yes. **A few steps in the right**

direction. I knew I wanted to do it. Again, because I knew what I wanted "to do" it helped me to say yes. I knew it would help me change lives. Looking back on it, I probably never would have asked to be the speaker. Thank you, God, for the push I needed. **A few steps in the right direction.** Are you starting to see it? Opportunities are always happening to get you where you need to be! Now, I just had to get over the fear of what others might think! Hopefully, you are starting to see the benefits of why it's important to take a chance on yourself from one opportunity to the next. The confidence gained from each opportunity slowly builds to help you say yes for the next opportunity. Now, how did fear try to cripple me? Let me explain. I had no PhD or no degree at all for that matter – just a college student still figuring it out! Most speakers I had seen were never students still in school. I primarily had only seen professors and administrators. This is what fear kept telling me! But getting back to always knowing what I wanted to do, I decided to take a chance on myself and I accepted the speaking engagement. It actually went very well and it did a lot for my confidence. I can remember the Director saying, "You gone have to save that speech!" Personally, I think the thing that mattered most was that I was growing more confident to say yes for me! **A few steps in the right direction!** To the person reading this – I know your experiences won't be exactly like mine and I don't want you to miss the point. Whatever it is you want to do, just give yourself a chance! Try it! Say yes! Go for it! You already know what's calling you, but you'll never get there if you hide your gift! Another thing, stop worrying about perfection! I noticed this in myself early on and I have often noticed this in others. People are often so afraid to make a mistake or to get it wrong! Why? Because it doesn't lend itself to perfection. Guess what? No one is perfect. Even a job well done is often not perfect! Remember that! **A few steps in the right direction!**

A quote that I use for my life is, "You are most special when being yourself." No one can do it like you. You are unique my friend! You don't have to aspire to be exactly like someone else because being you is enough. If for some reason your vision is not aligned in such a way, let me give you some tips on how to improve your vision:

- Pull off your dirty glasses!
- Learn to use the windshield wipers of your life!
- Get regular eye exams!

Dirty Glasses: You can't see any better today than you did on yesterday wearing the same old dirty pair of glasses; they are distorting your vision! What you should see for your life you don't see because your looking through filth such as, I'm not good enough, I don't have what it takes, I'm ugly, I'm too skinny, my left leg is bigger than my right leg! My neck is too short! My arms are too long, people laugh at my accent or voice! And on and on we go! Let me give you some advice! Stop it! Learn to see yourself as a gift to this world because that is what you are and the world is a better place when you believe in yourself and know you were meant to create positive change. You are not meant to live in mental, financial, spiritual, or visional poverty! The scripture says, **The thief cometh not but to steal and to kill and to destroy. I am come that they might have life, and that they might have it more abundantly.**[4] You believe that? If you do, then you have just taken **a few steps in the right direction!**

Windshield Wipers: You have to start using the windshield wipers of your life. You wouldn't drive a car with an excessively cracked windshield because you would not be able to see. A cracked windshield would hinder your vision. You also, wouldn't drive a car with an extremely dirty windshield. Imagine it is pouring rain and you decide not to use your windshield wipers. Not only are you going to hurt yourself but you are going to hurt others! You get it? It's bigger than just you. The wipers are there for us to wipe away anything that's getting in the way of our vision of being a greater blessing to others. So, to negative thinking-wipe it away! Find a mentor, pray, read encouraging books, and rid your life of people who perpetuate negative thinking. The lack of confidence-wipe it away! Learn to give yourself a chance. You too, can fulfill your dreams. Start small and keep working your way up if you need to. Yes, it will involve work but you can do it. Television producer, Shonda Rhimes says, "Dreams do not come true just because you dream them. It's hard work that makes things happen. It's hard work that creates change." And again, find people who believe in you and will help push you through the tough times. Comparing yourself to others-wipe that away too and drive into your destiny. There is no need to compare yourself. You have always been enough; you have always had the juice! **A few steps in the right direction!** It's time you believe it.

Eye Exams: Now, every now and then you're going to have to take inventory and this is what I mean about get an eye exam. Sometimes we all slip back and start living out a nightmare that we left a long time ago. Confront yourself by checking in with yourself. Yep, we all need to check in on ourselves from time to time. As rapper Ice Cube once said, "Check yo self before you wreck yo self." **A few steps in the right direction!** Don't ever be afraid to confront the problem or admit that something that you thought you had overcome is now again starring you in the face. It is imperative for you to be up front and honest with yourself. **A few steps in the right direction!**

My friend, your dreams are there for the taking! The choice is yours; however, you will make that choice depending on your vision. If you choose to see the rich and blessed dreams in front of you then you will work to have those dreams. If you choose nightmares then get ready to live a life of fear, cold sweats, and a lack of sleep. If I were you I would choose life! Choose your dreams!

Chapter 2 Reflection Questions

- What is it that you want to do? (focus on the actions, not an occupation)

- What occupations do you think fit the things you want to do? (there could be several)

- Are there areas where you need to pull off your dirty glasses? Use windshield wipers? What areas and how so?

KNOCK KNOCK

When adversity knocks at my door
I open that door
I step outside and I say, let's do it!
And that is all that needs to be said
It is the only thing that matters
Not, why are you here?
Or, for how long will you stay?
Not even, why are you picking on me?
I could care less
You see, I was built to last
Destined to handle these moments
I'm battle tested, victory invested
I'm a winner already, finish line crossed already
So, let's do it!
Oh yeah!
By the way
Adversity
Enjoy the view
Because I'm already through!

By: Kendrick Savage

3

STEPS

*My greatest fear is not living before I die,
to play everything so safe that even though
I had no risk I also enjoyed no reward*

– T.D. Jakes, Pastor and Author

My senior year at the University of Mississippi I gave a speech at an annual closing banquet for the Ronald E. McNair Program. Did you get that!? Once again, I decided to take a chance! I decided to give my gift a chance. **A few steps in the right direction.** The next morning, I had a conversation with my mother, and showed her the appreciation gifts I was presented with. My mother, who never stepped foot on a college campus, expressed to me that she was proud of me. She thought the future was going to be very bright for me. It didn't occur to me then, but I realized later that she could see something I couldn't. I say that because I was only focused on the night before. I couldn't see past the speech. Perhaps, what seemed like a secret to me, she already knew. I later realized my mother knew the power of God. She believed in the scripture, **Trust in the Lord with all thine heart; and lean not unto thine own understanding. In all thy ways acknowledge him, and he shall direct thy paths.**[1] You see, my mother also knew the power of steps, steps in the right direction. Scripture says, **Behold the fowls of the air: for they sow not, neither do they reap, nor gather into barns: yet your heavenly Father feedeth them. Are ye not much better than they?**[2] Whatever you set out to do will not be easy, but difficulty can be a blessing! I have learned that you don't let adversity break you, you let it make you! **A few steps in the right direction!**

Have you ever sat on your porch and watched birds? They never seem to be concerned about anything, they just keep moving. They use what God has given them; and they keep pressing forward each day, and worrying is not the goal but striving is. They press forward using their ability to fly and soar.

My friends, stop worrying, rise from your bed and get up to do your best. Isn't that what we tell little kids? We say, just do your best, that's all I ask of you and I'll be proud of you. However, when it comes to us, the adults, we sometimes forget that. So, you give your best and I pray you have love ones around you that let you know that it is enough. If you don't, I'll tell you now that I am proud of you and all I ask of you is to do your best! One day you will look up, and you will have done more than you ever imagined. Let me share a worry moment from my life. When I first started college, my thoughts were endless in reference to this question: "What is my purpose?" I was looking for this one big thing! Where was it? It was such a stress for me! One day God spoke to me and told me, purpose is daily! Every day is filled with purpose! Stop worrying about this one big thing! This one great job or great relationship. Your job is to do your best with each step and it will ultimately lead to multiple great opportunities in multiple areas of your life. Again, purpose is daily! **A few steps in the right direction**. Meaning, you'll meet who you meet because it's on purpose, you will help a particular person because It's on purpose, and it will be on purpose when you are compelled to action. Why do I have a passion to mentor? Because it's purpose! Why might you be reading this book? It's purpose! Now, you may have something that brings you more attention and more notoriety one day – that one big thing! And that will be purpose too, but don't miss the everyday, sometimes seemingly insignificant moments that represent purpose. Don't miss your steps! **A few steps in the right direction!** So, it is with these words I would like to discuss the title of this chapter, steps!

I remember reading once about Will Smith where his father tore down a 16 feet high and 40 feet wide wall in front of his shop. His father told him and his brother that they were to rebuild the wall for the summer. It took them more than just the summer to build the wall. But I read, once they finished the wall his father said, "Now, don't you all ever tell me there's something you can't do." Now, from that Will says he learned that, "I do not have to build a perfect wall today. I just have to lay a perfect brick. Just one brick dude." You don't have to make a living in one day! Sometimes your dreams are not realized in one day either! Just keep stepping! One step at a time, one decision at a time! Any journey is full of steps. **A few steps in the right direction!**

I once expressed to a friend of mine that I just didn't know if I'd ever make my dreams a reality. I knew deep down what I wanted, what I thought I could become, and the difference I felt I could make, but getting there was the issue. I was afraid that one day I would leave this earth with my story incomplete. Part of it was me, afraid to step out on my dreams. The other part of it was I just had no vision on how to bring all of these dreams together or if I would ever reach my goals. There I was staring into the future and I knew there was an opportunity to do something great. A moment of clarity happened for me one day. I attended a seminar by an elderly, wise, and experienced motivational speaker. I asked him about all of his achievements and how did he make them happen. I remember him saying, "I like to think of life as wearing a big crown and you spend your life growing into it." In that moment, I realized I already had the crown! The dreams were mine! You see, in that moment I realized accomplishing anything takes time – sometimes lots of time! What I didn't realize was that he was explaining to me the power of steps! Another moment of clarity was realizing I had to stop thinking about results, stop thinking about what could be one day and create what will be today! **A few steps in the right direction!** I am thankful for the revelations, they have left me with many lessons and there are a couple in particular that I will pull out:

Opportunities: The first lesson is to take advantage of your opportunities. I need you to get comfortable with taking advantage of your opportunities. This, my friend, is **a few steps in the right direction!** I believe now that accepting those leadership positions in college in part helped me to become more relaxed in front of people when I had to speak. I have always been a little too nervous to get in front of anyone. But after stepping out on faith and going through the rigors of standing in front of people during my earlier leadership positions I became more equipped to handle the attention of being in front of a crowd. This led me later in my undergraduate career to form my own poetry recital club along with a friend. If there is anything from it all I've learned, it is not to worry about all the things you want to become. Taking the small steps will get you there! This is how you enjoy the journey. Another important lesson I learned concerning steps is that it's the small steps that will get you there.

Appreciate the small steps: Some people don't want a job because they can't start at CEO. Some people want nice houses, cars, and expensive bank accounts but because they can't get it in one day, to them it's too much of a hassle to even do the small stuff which will ultimately get them there. I will say that again, which will ultimately get them there! The first day we want to be the CEO not the guy that no one knows, we want a mansion and not the trailer, we want a BMW not a CWW-Crank When It WANTS! I am not saying we shouldn't have these things but sometimes it takes time and for some of us it's longer than others. I can recall listening to interview given by women's college basketball coach Vic Shaefer. He said, "Some of us wish that we could take a nap and wake up champions." That would be nice! But it doesn't happen that way. But none the less you will reach your destination my friend just hang in there and keep pushing. I have learned this because as I look over my life it has been the small steps whether I realized it or not which has led me to some of my ultimate goals. Remember the elderly motivational speaker I mentioned? Before he left that day, he looked at me and said, "Kendrick you have book in you!" **A few steps in the right direction!** So, here we are! Appreciate those small steps! Again, God is always speaking! Practicing my poetry before my own club led to me winning a poetry slam one semester and being the opening act for some professional poets! Now, I couldn't have just started out displaying my gift on that large of a scene but it all happened in perfect timing. Reciting poetry to my own club allowed me to take those small steps in helping me become a better poet and even having more confidence in the things that I wrote. So, when opportunity came knocking in the form of a competition I was prepared, prepared because of the small steps! **A few steps in the right direction!**

When I was a kid, my peers and even some grown-ups would ask me, why do you walk slow? Why do you talk slow? And if they asked me a question and I took time to think it over, then I heard, why does it take you so long to respond? Now, when you are kid you haven't lived enough life to know that it's ok to be just who God made you! It wasn't like I woke up and decided I was going to be this way, it's who I've always been. I think it was experiences like this that caused me to compare myself a lot early on. Truth be told, I still get these same comments every now and then. How do I handle it as an adult? American writer Audre Lorde says, "If you don't define yourself for yourself, then you'll be crunched into other peoples' fantasies of you and eaten alive." I know who I am and I rest in who God made me to be and I keep it stepping without worry. Now, that doesn't mean I disrespect people or their time. I don't do that, but I am myself. Growing up, I remember a lady at my church once told me, "Don't worry about people rushing you to a destination, you will get there on time, and maybe in better shape than them." **A few steps in the right direction!**

Chapter 3 Reflection Questions

- How can you take one step closer to your goals and dreams today? Just one step.

- Do you have trouble taking small steps instead of huge steps? Why?

- Have there been things that have been said to you that are hindering you from taking the steps necessary to accomplish your goals? How can you overcome these comments and/or actions?

FLIGHT SCHOOL

I've always known I had wings
What a special gift to have
Having wings that is
You see, I was graced that way
Put on this place that way
I inspire the nation this way
Counting blessings, not problems
Problems show up, no worries
Fasting shows up, no hurries
No fear is needed, Prayer gets repeated
I stay poise to the noise
I just plant my feet
And I stay ready
So that when the rain comes
I take flight

By: Kendrick Savage

4

WHAT HAPPENED? YOU HAPPENED!

> If you want to be successful, you have to jump, there's no way around it. When you jump, I can assure you that your parachute will not open right away. But if you do not jump, your parachute will never open. If you're safe, you'll never soar!
>
> - Steve Harvey, Comedian, Radio and Game Show Host

So many people never make it off their own front porch of life. Now, we have no problem watching others - celebrities, athletes, actors and other popular figures. We watch them excel at their crafts and bask in the glow of their accomplishments. Guess what? So could you and so should you. Get used to this word – YOU, YOU, YOU, and YOU again! There is a world out there that needs your touch! A world that needs your gift and talent! What am I saying? Go make your mark! Believe in yourself and go make a difference. Stop being afraid, stop comparing yourself to others. You, and only you are enough! You happened because the world needs you as a difference maker. A problem solver. I came across a quote by the Dalai Lama, "If you think you are too small to make a difference, try sleeping with a mosquito." **A few steps in the right direction!** I don't even have to tell you how that situation turned out, LOL! Mosquitoes might be small, but they have not an ounce of fear! Ok, no excuses! Go make it happen! Actress, author and vegan food star Tabitha Brown shares these encouraging words in her book *Feeding The Soul*, "We are no longer going to dim our lights or hide our shine just to accommodate someone else's limited thinking." Get off the front porch, open the yard gate, remove the boundaries from your mind, and go make some noise! **A few steps in the right direction!**

We all have a sound! Some of us are loud, some of us are quiet. Have you ever been around someone who is loud? Yes, you have. I'm sure of it. I know I have. Equally so, you've been around someone really quiet as well. What would life be if everyone was loud? A headache for one! What would life be if everyone was quiet? Another headache from trying to read minds! What would life be without dogs, cats, fish, flowers, horses? Are you starting to understand? What would the world be without you? That is the ultimate question. The world needs your sound! You may be quiet but I find most quiet people are very observant. So, when they do talk they actually have something to say. They may ponder things that a talker probably wouldn't take time to ponder. Suppose you are loud, you talk a lot. It's possible you miss small details. However, we need the talkers because we cannot play the quiet game forever. Whatever excuse you have been using that's keeping you from believing in yourself and believing the world needs you stops now!

Why do we believe we are not needed, that no one sees us? Think about a full band. The trumpet does not do it all. The flute can't carry the whole band! They work together understanding that each sound is not to be compared but is unique and brings a special sound that no other instrument can bring. So, look at it this way: You are an instrument and instruments make sounds. The problem is some of us don't know what kind of instrument we are. Ask God! **A few steps in the right direction!** Talk to people you trust. Pay attention to what makes you full, what makes you feel alive. What are you doing when you feel at peace? In the zone? In your element? Some of us are so mixed up. We are trying to be a drum when we know we are a flute!

Be yourself! You are most special when being yourself. **A few steps in the right direction!** Put the world on notice my friend that you are here to stay! That you were born with purpose and promise! You were born to win! Born to shine! God has a purpose for your life. It is purpose that you are reading this; it is purpose for you to meet certain people. Don't you ever give up! It is imperative that you know who YOU are and that you view yourself in the most positive light! In his song, "Don't Forget Who You Are", actor and rapper, Common says

> "Beautiful baby I love you, baby
> Pray these words may hug you, baby
> Look into the mirror and say "I love you" daily
> Remember your light when the world seems shady
> You're born with it, adorned with it
> A gift to the world, go on, give it
> Fearlessly made, no need to be afraid
> Angels are with you, the path is laid
> Waning thoughts of you being the star
> Truly you'll shine by seeing who you are
> Reflections of you, reflections of me
> The beauty more than any eyes can see

A few steps in the right direction! Remember, you have been placed on this earth for a reason. You never know, there may be someone five years from now that is going to need you. All because YOU happened and decided not to give up! You will tutor someone in a difficult subject because YOU happened! A life will come out of depression into prosperity because YOU happened! Your family will realize there is a way out of poverty because YOU happened! If I were asked, "Why are you writing this book?" I would say, "It's simple, because I happened!" But I would not be here if it were not for God and all the people who took the time to do what I want to do for you. To help you realize you're potential deserves to be out front and center! Go get it! I love the words of Viola Davis from the L'OREAL commercial:

"You're worth it, three words we have all heard at least a thousand times, right. You're worth it but do you really understand what that means? It's a beautiful reminder to us all that we have worth, you have reason and rarity, there is value in each and every one of us including you, that is precious even on the days you might not feel it, you never depreciate in value those words are there to remind you, so to all those watching who feel like that or have ever felt like that focus on what I'm about to say, and repeat after me. I'm worth it! Ok? Maybe that felt great or perhaps that felt weird. Let's go again. First take a deep breath and let it out. Forget the naysayers and silence the critics, even if the harshest words are the ones you say to yourself, do not doubt yourself and this time speak it louder, really loud! I'm worth it! And the next time you hesitate before going after something you want, the next time you blush and brush off a compliment, the next time you doubt your place in the world, in the workplace, in your home, or in your own skin, say these words to yourself. I'm worth it! And I know you will always say it like you mean it. I'm worth it because you are and always will be. Got that? " **A few steps in the right direction!**

Chapter 4 Reflection Questions

- What do you think is keeping you from soaring?

- How would your life look if you truly understood that you are the gift?

- What's out there that you need to put your touch on?

SHOES WITH SOULS

How many can say that they have shoes with
souls? Souls of new and souls of old,
Souls so incredibly intellectual and representing gold
These shoes of souls undeniably are impeccable,
climbing mountaintops, having dreams like King
and like Rosa we'll stay parked in our seat.
I'll stay planted never taking for granted the
people I greet, the food I sit to eat,
The buses I can ride in stride to go vote at polls
all because of these shoes with souls
I'll give you another clue it ain't all about you,
but more so what you make it through.
Because its shoes with souls that take it to another level,
like the ones before us you better know it's several.
I got proof to believe, I've seen some deceived
But I must live through the old because they got shoes with souls.

By: Kendrick Savage

5

SHOES WITH SOULS

> Ease is a greater threat to progress than hardship
>
> - Denzel Washington, American Actor

Having shoes with souls is a very interesting concept. When I introduce this idea to people verbally they automatically think I mean shoes with "soles". But I am not speaking of the sole on the bottom of your shoe. Shoes with souls mean those who have walked through the fire of life and have been burned a couple of times, but they were not consumed. Shoes with souls means those who have started the climb to the top of Mount Forever realizing that though the dream seems impossible, they are still on the side of that mountain climbing to reach the top. It means to swim the Nile River while learning to swim along the way! It is a deep concept that causes you to realize in order for you to stand the test of time in your walk you are going to have to develop shoes with souls that have a spirit of "relentlessness," that have a "spirit of go get it," that have a spirit of today "I will make it!" Possessing this type of spirit will be **a few steps in the right direction!**

I am a much stronger person today than I was years ago. We all wish for roads that are straight and have no twist and turns in life. However, this is not always the case. There will be trials, tribulations, and tests. You can call them the three T's, but they will happen. It is a certainty that we will all experience those things that in the end will cause us to stretch and earn our wings. What am I trying to say? Having shoes with souls is a good thing! Now, what we go through to obtain these shoes will more than likely never feel good. Adversity produces greatness, it won't feel like, but you can't be scared of it! **A few steps in the right direction!** The realization is that you cannot have something for nothing! There is no food on the table if you do not work. No grade of "A" happens without hard work. You see opportunities are seldom loss to setbacks, but more so to those that sit down. **A few steps in the right direction!** Going through hardships of today mean making life a little easier in the future. The bible says, **For I reckon that the sufferings of this present time are not worthy to be compared with the glory which shall be revealed in us.**[1] Jesus reminds us, **These things I have spoken unto you, that in me ye might have peace. In the world ye shall have tribulation: but be of good cheer; I have overcome the world.**[2] The world is going to throw its everlasting daggers at you and smile its deceitful grin in your face, but we must trust in the one who has already overcome this world. God is our refuge, and He is the one that allows you to climb Mount Forever, to swim the Nile, and to develop your shoes with souls. For about 6 years after I was born, my family lived with my grandparents. We stayed so far in the country that the school bus would not come to our house to pick us up. We had to either walk to and from the pick-up spot or get my parents to take us if they were able to. However, on a lot of mornings my brother and I were able to get rides to catch the bus but rarely in the afternoon, which meant we walked. When I first started walking this long road it was very difficult because my brother was older, had longer legs, and he was more experienced with this journey and could leave me at any time. I had to earn my wings. I had to earn my shoes! I thank God for the training session! **A few steps in the right direction!**

    Soon I was able to keep up better and feel more secure that I could make it home safely. I was able to run pretty fast after it was over with because I was trying to keep up with my brother. So when he decided he wanted to run the distance home guess what, I had to as well or get left! My point is that initially the distance we had to walk or run seemed ridiculous and to be honest it was. However, in the end we both learned to manage and we became stronger, faster, and better at navigating our way through a long journey that was filled with woods with any and everything in them! My friend's life is a journey that will present many roads as choices. Some of these roads will be taken and some will not. There will be challenges along the way, but you must realize that you will be a much stronger, equipped and skilled individual if you stay the course and develop your shoes with souls. Another thing – Your level of strength will always be met by the proper level of resistance! **A few steps in the right direction!** This means that the challenge in front of you is never more than the strength, wisdom, ability, or knowledge that you already possess. I can hear some of the old folks in my life right now saying, "You got that right!" LOL. **A few steps in the right direction!**

I am reminded of a story I read about a man that Jesus told to push a gigantic rock. Well, the man pushed the rock for what seemed liked weeks and months. He pushed as hard as he could and as diligent as he could. He was obedient to God telling him to push the rock. Finally, tired and frustrated, the man asked God, "Why is this rock not moving. I have been pushing it and pushing it and still no progress!" God simply replied to him by saying, "I never said the rock was going to move nor did I ask you to move the rock." I only said to push. Frustrated the man replied, "Well what was the point of this?" God says to him, "Even though you did what I said and that rock did not move take a look at your hands, your arms, and your back at how much stronger they are and how much strength you have built." My friends developing shoes with souls will cause you to endure some great challenges some in which you will feel your failing but rest assure you are prospering. The bible says, **In all labour there is profit: but the talk of the lips tendeth only to penury**.[3] At any point in time if you take a look back at history it is very evident that many of our civil rights leaders such as Martin Luther King Jr, Rosa Parks, and so forth had shoes with souls. It doesn't stop there because some of us live with parents and grandparents that have shoes with souls.

All of these remarkable and deeply rooted individuals have been blown by the wind of negativity; they have been rained on by poverty and have been snowed in at some point by a blanket of hopelessness that appeared around them. There is one thing that they have in common. They learned how to trust that the situation was gone be alright in spite of what they saw in front of them. **A few steps in the right direction!** In the book of JOB, the scripture says, **Though he slay me, yet will I trust in him . . .** [4] You have to be able to persevere through the difficult moments. Friends you have to be able to lift that blanket of hopelessness and see the sunshine that is to come. The scripture says, **Rejoicing in hope; patient in tribulation; continuing instant in prayer;** [5] I have learned that in every situation there is always something to rejoice in, now you might not look at it as important at the time but it is indeed a rejoicing moment. Then, as you learn to rejoice in the face of adversity that will give you hope. But tribulation will still come and it is then that you need to be patient. All the while you're dealing with this turbulent situation and all the tribulation is going on you must continually stay in prayer. I am speaking to those of you who are overcomers and might not even know it. Buckle down and as your ride becomes bumpy make sure you hold on tight! I am proud of you! I rejoice with you! And I thank God for you!

Make sure to reach back because there are shoes with souls in the pipeline waiting to be made and you have been called upon to help that brother or sister. Make me proud! You will be elated in the end for never giving in to that ever present feeling of laziness, lack of faith, and incapability. Hang on my love ones your shoe deal is on the way but it's earned through a relentless attitude fueled by perseverance and a determination that's unshakable.

Chapter 5 Reflection Questions

- How do you handle difficulty? Is it with ease or distress? Is it with confidence?

- How do you envision adversity making you stronger?

- In what areas have difficulty made you stronger mentally, physically, spiritually?

- How can you show the next generation how to persevere through the difficult moments?

IT'S JUST THAT SIMPLE

Do you want to change the world?
Do you want the sick to be healed?
The depressed to be encouraged?
The lost to be saved?
It's simple…
Dedicate yourself to love
And when you get tired
Dedicate yourself some more!
But to do that, you got to do this one thing
Stop being so judgmental!
We are out of time
You see, without love
You're the man doing five to ten
Without love
Your worth is now based on trends
And don't be so quick to say what you wouldn't do
Because without love, it could've been you
Could've been you sleeping under a bridge
Could've been you with no food in the fridge
It could've been you left feeling alone
And it could've been you abandoning your home
So, the message is simple
The message is clear
Choose love over judgement
Choose love over fear

By: Kendrick Savage

6

MORE THAN A SHELL

I love to give. I've been a giver all my life

– Tyler Perry, Actor, Director, and Writer

As a young boy growing up, my parents taught me one of the most valuable lessons that I could ever learn. They taught me the importance of giving to others. It did not matter who crossed our door step in the Savage family they were going to be respected. It was expected! My parents did not see it any other way. **A few steps in the right direction!** I can remember on a number of occasions people would visit our home that you could tell were having a hard time with life. The amazing thing about it was I still saw my parents treat them equally and with respect! The bible reads, **For there is no respect of persons with God.**[1] If they were hungry my parents fed them, and if they needed a friend my parents were there. This was hard to understand as a young boy. It wasn't that I didn't believe in helping people, it's just that at that time I only felt like we should help certain people, not all necessarily. I was wrong. **A few steps in the right direction!** I did not have the capacity at that age to understand that giving must be extended beyond anything that seems to be a barrier. I also didn't understand that if I lived long enough that I too would have my difficult moments! That, my friend, is life! So, it is with that I start this chapter.

Now, as a young man, I find giving as one of the most important things that I have ever been the recipient of. From my parents and through the love of God I have been able to and still learning to be a better giver myself. The bible says, **Give and it shall be given unto you; good measure, pressed down, and shaken together, and running over, shall men give into you bosom. For with the same measure that ye mete withal it shall be measured to you again.**[2] I recall another occasion as a teenager. I was helping my dad with some welding once and we just could not get it right. We were destroying the pipe that we were trying to weld together. So, I took a break and I left the house for about an hour. Now, upon my return I noticed there was a man, not my dad, under our carport. He was now helping my dad. Yes, I'd seen this man before here and there. But every time I saw him he seemed to be in a state of unproductivity and possibly suffering from his own vices. It did not take the man no more than fifteen minutes to do what Dad and I had been trying to do for what seemed like forever. Now, after it was all over my dad said to me, "If people only looked at him from the outside they would never know what he is capable of." I remember thinking, "Yeah that's true."

So, that day my dad taught me a valuable lesson on how not to judge people by the way they look on the outside, and he also taught me that everybody has something to give even the man that you think is only a drunk or the woman that you think is only a drug addict. There is another pivotal occasion with my dad that I can remember. I can remember coming home from school one day and found my mom and dad sitting in the kitchen, speaking with a lady who was a friend of one of our relatives. She had been having a hard time in life for years and you could see it, and it was clearly due to her own vices. Then again, you never know a person's story. Do you? **A few steps in the right direction!** Perhaps that's the lesson here. Let me continue. Typical of my parents, they were always nice to her if she visited. Standing there watching, my dad must could see the displeasing look on my face and decided to grab me before my look would cause any disrespect or harm to this lady. I can remember this like yesterday. My dad simply said to me, "Kendrick, come on let's go to the back." He took me to his room, sat beside me on his bed, and spoke to me calmly. He said to me, "Kendrick, I understand how you feel but we cannot mistreat people. It does not matter if they are going through hard times. You must always show respect to people and not approach them in a way that makes them feel less." Thanks dad! **A few steps in the right direction!** Our giving is the one thing that just might help them get back on track. And sometimes giving means – just give people another chance! **A few steps in the right direction.** And no, I'm not saying it is our job and ours only to get them back on track. I am saying that when the time comes and they want to do better, please don't let it be said that you were the one that held them back with judgement and had no time to give to them. Your giving is just that important. **A few steps in the right direction!** There is a quote by Dalai Lama that reads, "Our primary goal in life is to help others. And if we cannot help them, then at the very least do not hurt them." My giving is not where I want it to be and I'm constantly working to improve it. I am constantly pushing myself to get better at being obedient to the Holy Spirit and becoming a better listener. The reason for this is that God will guide us to individuals that need help, if we are listening. Sometimes they will cross our path unexpectedly to us, but expectantly from God. We have to be sensitive enough to God to see them. I mean really see them and understand you have been blessed with a moment to give!

 I remember one night in college I was on my way to bible study. I needed to stop by the bookstore real quick and make my way to the church. But on the way into the bookstore I bumped into a friend. We started talking and I realized I was doing most of the listening. I could tell they needed someone. I checked my watch a few times and starting wondering if I should tell them I had to go or should I stay there and listen. It was there in that moment I realized I was being given a moment to give! Maybe God wanted me to be there with that person. I ended up staying and until this day I honestly believe it was where I was supposed to be. And it wasn't easy for me to do because I did not like missing bible study. However, this is what I mean about being sensitive to God. Sometimes you are needed somewhere else. Sometimes purpose calls for you to give what you've learned. **A few steps in the right direction!** For anyone who has experienced anything close to success in his or her life there is no way you can say you did it on your own. Somebody gave to you; somebody thought enough of you to put time aside to help you along. As a teacher I remind my students often that I am here to help them reach their full potential if that's what they want. My life has been so immensely blessed by those that took time to give to me. There are so many people listed in my acceptance speech of being thankful! It would be a shame for me to not extend this same help and time to others. To all the givers of this world, continue to give and give some more. The world needs your flavor – that way that you give! Those of you who feel you don't have time, don't feel like being bothered, or you just have an image to maintain, it is not all about you! Did you get that? I'll say it again, it's not all about you! We all need help, even you! So, join the movement! As civil rights activist John Lewis once said, "Never be afraid to make some noise and get in trouble, good trouble necessary trouble." This, my friend, is good work, it's good trouble! **A few steps in the right direction.**

Ladies and gentlemen the world needs your love. The world needs your smile. The world needs your touch. The world needs your poetic mind. The world needs your giftedness in academics, church, barbershops, schools, committees, kitchens, and at home. You see, giving is the best of things. How do I know? Jesus says, **For God so loved the world, that he gave his only begotten Son, that whosoever believeth in him should not perish, but have everlasting life.**[3] Remember, you have a choice. My encouragement to you is to always choose to give. Someone is definitely going to need you. There is a quote that says, **"To the world you may be one person, but to one person you just might be the world."** Will you give yourself an opportunity?

Looking back over my journey so far I'm beyond thankful to those that helped me! Thank you! I think about what if they had chosen not to spend that extra time with me? What if they had chosen to write me off? I am grateful to God because these individuals did none of that. They spent time with me and help me work through issues, they made telephone calls, visits, and encouraged me to do exactly what they knew was on the inside of me and that was to exercise the greatness that God has given to me. I have been inspired! I have been taught and encouraged to do the same. I could earn 100 degrees, a big bank account, and have 20 unique vehicles, but it won't mean a thing If I didn't help somebody else. **A few steps in the right direction.**

Chapter 6 Reflection Questions

- Do you have trouble giving to others? Why or why not?

- What is easiest for you to give? And why? (advice, time, gifts...)

- What would stop you from taking time out for someone else if you knew it would change their life?

DREAM BELIEVER

The reason I have dreams is to give other people dreams
Dreams that make you king
And dreams that crown you queen
Red carpet dreams
Dreams that shine
Dreams like mine
Dreams so rare
They are one of a kind
Dreams that create abundance!
Dreams that spotlight joy!
Dreams that uplift humanity!
And dreams that are hard to ignore!
You are what you dream!
You become what you believe!
So remember, whatever dream you believe
Will be the dream you achieve!

By: Kendrick Savage

7

THE RED CARPET

> If you want some big stuff, then you better have faith because money ain't enough
>
> – Canton Jones, Gospel Artist

When one thinks about the red carpet most of us probably imagine movie stars, lights, and cameras. We think about reporters asking movie stars WHO they are wearing instead of WHAT they are wearing! It is a glorious occasion where all the glamorous people we support on the big and small screen congregate at one time and are treated like royalty. The reality is that so many of us watch this great event and it never occurs to us that we should be on that same red carpet. Now, understand you don't have to be a movie star to be on the red carpet. I am only using this as a metaphor. The red carpet in this scenario symbolizes confidence, respect, positivity, greatness, extraordinary leadership, and the love of God. So, when I talk about us being on the red carpet I mean how you view yourself, how you treat yourself, what you believe about your life, and what you can accomplish. Check. Your. Mentality. Simply put, you have to have a red-carpet mentality; you have to have a red-carpet perspective about yourself. **A few steps in the right direction!**

It is important that you know your worth. You deserve to be on the red carpet - there is something about you that lights up a room, something about you that is needed, and something about you that people love. Things as simple as the jokes you tell, the way you dress, how your character permeates throughout the work office, or even your infectious smile. However, that does not happen without the proper mentality. It does not happen without the proper belief and treatment of yourself.

The bible says, **Ye are of God, little children, and have overcome them: because greater is he that is you, than he that is in the world.**[1] Don't let past experiences rob you of what you deserve or sway you from feeling better about yourself. My friend, the red carpet mentality is a must. It is the best of thinking. Not conceited, but humble, and not belittling, but respectful. A red carpet mentality does not accept defeat, financial poverty, or a defeating attitude. A red carpet mentality seeks what is true and embraces it as a great way to live.

I learned a long time ago in college that it is so easy to wake up with negativity on your mind. It can be so subtle - groans about the new day, dreading all that you have to do, and who you have to be around. It's so easy to think about all the responsibilities. Have you ever felt so much pressure that it felt like the world was on top of you? Sometimes it can feel like there is no point in even getting up from the bed. Be careful, those very things you are groaning about could be your blessing. My encouragement is for you to embrace the red carpet mentality and treat yourself as such. But sometimes you can be on the red carpet and not even know it. That's right! You are blessed. You have achieved goals and dreams, the love of friends, and the love of your community. But because it comes with so much responsibility and effort to maintain we can become blind to the blessing and in full awareness of the responsibility. To the person reading this book – don't forget to have some fun too! Stay balanced! **A few steps in the right direction!** My encouragement to you is to never quit and don't ever allow yourself to develop anything other than a red-carpet mentality. Start expecting people to be nice to you, start expecting great things to happen to your life. **A few steps in the right direction.** Go on and dance your dance, smile for the cameras, dress your best and enjoy the show – That's the red carpet mentality.

Chapter 7 Reflection Questions

- What is keeping you from a red-carpet mentality?

- Are you struggling to think positive when you wake up? Why?

- What are three things you can do (and know you will do) to start each day off with a more positive mindset?

MY FATHERS ARE GREAT

It is my Father in heaven who blesses my father on earth
To have and to hold me, since birth
It is not a mistake that He blesses my father to be the man that he is
To give gifts like love and protection to his kids
And He blesses my father to be able to relate to this very date
To the trials and tribulations of his offspring
Because my fathers are great
You see, without the Father in heaven
There would be no father on earth
Without the Father in Heaven dad would
Have died and left this earth
Without the Father in heaven there would be no me
To experience the love of a father, you see
I know that I am covered, I know that I am seen
I know that I am protected
I know that He is King
So, the storms can come, but my will shall never break!
Because of my fathers, my fathers are great!

By: Kendrick Savage

8

THE TESTIMONY

> My mother told me 'fore she passed away
> Said, son, when I'm gone, don't forget to pray
> 'Cause there'll be hard times, hard
> times, woah, yeah, yeah
> Who knows better than I?
>
> – Hard Times, by Ray Charles

I remember being a kid growing up listening to older people give testimonies. **A few steps in the right direction!** Some were very dramatic and humorous while others were very sad and heartfelt. However, the one thing they all shared was the belief that God could do the miraculous and He is always in control. We all have testimonies, regardless of how big or small they appear. These testimonies can be very liberating and can provide faith for everything we face in our life. Testimonies for me were always a thing for older people - until one particular summer.

    I was out of school and ready to have a great summer. The days were just as pretty and hot as any other summer in the state of Mississippi. My summer was just as busy as any of my previous summers. The upcoming fall I would be starting my junior year in high school; I was getting closer to being a senior and becoming a senior meant soon I would be walking across a stage. Graduating meant a lot to my parents, and I was ready to make them proud. There was something that happened to my family that summer though that would change our lives forever. My dad got sick! I awoke one summer morning to find that my older brother had to take my father to the hospital because he was experiencing some stomach pains. I shrugged it off, no big deal, prior to this point I'd never really seen my dad with anything other than a cold. I thought to myself the day before, everything had been fine; I was in the yard with my dad just yesterday I thought and nothing was wrong. Well, as the afternoon approached my brother returned home but my dad was not in the car. He gave us the news that my dad had to stay in the hospital. Suddenly, things became real! Things got real scary! Like I said, I'd never really seen my dad sick. I was scared. My sister and I visited my dad a few hours later. I will never forget the experience of walking into the hospital room and seeing my dad lying in that bed. I could see his stomach moving and you could hear it making noises. Those of you who are reading this may think nothing of that, but once I finish you will understand. I was scared for him and the entire family. I immediately started crying, but turned away because I wanted to be strong for my sister. When we left the hospital we both had no idea what was going to happen. We knew our dad was sick but we thought maybe it will be a week kind of thing and he will come home.

Dad wouldn't make it home until about two months later. It was about two days later that the doctors moved my dad from a regular room to the intensive care unit. It was hard seeing this. I could not stand to see my father sick like that. It was new to me. Every child wants their parents to always feel well and to be in good spirits but for once in my life one of my parents were extremely sick. Then it was only a short while later we received news that my father's kidneys had stopped functioning so he was being transported to another hospital. Things were looking worse and worse at the time. My father's condition kept getting worse. He started dealing with a lot of organ failure. Eventually, he would be put on life support. One Sunday while in church my uncle showed up and my sister and I knew it was bad news. He came to get us out of church to see my dad. Before we ever left church my sister and I just cried in front of my uncle and some of the members in church. A horrible feeling for young kids.

I did not know what to believe. Were the doctors going to tell me my dad was about to die? The whole car ride was dreadful because of random thoughts. My uncle received the call from the doctors who were saying we needed to come and see him because he might pass away. Once we got there they even told us that my dad may be brain dead. Can you believe this? Playing in the yard one day and about three weeks later, brain dead? What? I remember standing there beside my brother feeling destroyed. The man who was our hero and protector was sick beyond measure. The whole time my dad was in the hospital his body was in such a bad shape until they kept him sedated. He was always out of it. So, it was as if he was in a coma for about two months. At the time I had a mentor in my life who suggested that I read scripture to my father. **A few steps in the right direction!** Every time I visited my father, I read the following scripture, **Hast thou not known? Hast thou not heard, that the everlasting God, the Lord, the Creator of the ends of the earth, fainteth not, neither is weary? There is no searching of his understanding. He giveth power to the faint; and to them that have no might he increaseth strength. Even the youths shall faint and be weary, and the young men shall utterly fall: But they that wait upon the Lord shall renew their strength; they shall mount up with wings as eagles; they shall run, and not be weary; and they shall walk, and not faint.**[2] I would read this by his bedside every time I went to see him because I wanted my father to mount up with wings like eagles and get out of that hospital bed! I wanted him to see daylight; I wanted him to see his son graduate from high school. I wanted my dad back because I loved him. I mentioned at the beginning of this chapter that I almost lost one of my parents. After all of that, my dad survived! It was truly a miracle! I mean he did a total 180 degrees. It seemed like out of nowhere he started getting better and better.

For me, there was no other explanation other than God was the author! **A few steps in the right direction!** Imagine seeing your dad on life support and then out of nowhere being able to go home. And I say "out of nowhere" because the doctors made it seem like he was going to die. They didn't really give us much hope of any kind. This is why somebody, anybody, has to have faith that the contrary can happen! **A few steps in the right direction!** It was a long and slow process but my dad left that hospital with everything working! And he was never ever brain dead! I remember being a young kid and hearing older people say, "God gets the last say so" well now I understand. I thank God for what he did for my family and for my father! Not only did my dad come home but he was able to continue being the hard worker he always was. He will always be a hero. God will never leave you nor will He forsake you. I don't care what you may be going through in your life. God is a healer! God is a keeper! God is your everlasting strength! He is the beginning of your day and the end of your day! Don't you ever give up this fight! The bible says, **Have not I commanded thee? Be strong and of a good courage; be not afraid, neither be thou dismayed; for the LORD thy God is with thee withersoever thou goest.**[1]

I wanted to tell this story because I have had many challenges in my life. I will admit that experiencing challenges is hard and can really test your ability to keep moving. But after witnessing that miracle, everything else I tend to face in life has paled in comparison. For the rest of my life there is nothing that I believe can destroy me because I have seen the lowest of a moment become the highest. So, when someone asks me, do you believe in miracles? My answer is yes! God is always capable of taking a situation and showing you He's God. He is a lover of His people! I know because God brought my father through and showed me that He will always work my situation out. He has been blessing me ever since to climb the mountains that seem to be too slippery to climb, to jump hurdles that never go away, and to conquer battles that are won by way of the Holy Spirit! My dad has always taught me to embrace who I am. He also taught me to embrace my last name. You got to have some bite on the inside! You got to have a little fire! Somewhere deep on the inside of me is a beast – and I mean that in the best of ways. **A few steps in the right**

direction! My dad, very early in life always tried to instill that in me. In other words if you have to scratch, bite, kick, claw, and jump your way to victory then you better do so! It is God that makes the impossible possible, it is God that can heal any broken family, and it is God that can take your Mount-Everest problem and cut it down to amount to nothing! Some people ask me why I keep going and this is why! Because I have witnessed the bottom of a pit and I have seen God come down to the pit and bring my father from a place that some people may have thought only death resides, but God who his rich in mercy and has a surplus of love thought differently. Some people say that the apple does not fall too far from the tree. So, the same drive and tenacity that my father has is on the inside of me and even though we might use it to do different things, the most important thing is that it is recognized and used to help overcome the many obstacles that come our way.

This chapter is very personal to me because many years later I still cannot tell the story of my dad without almost crying! But I am not sad at all, if anything I am so grateful my father made it through. If there is anything I would want someone to take from this chapter it is to know that God can fix your situation. Most importantly if you come to him He will be right by your side through it all. May God bless you and may you let Him ignite that everlasting fire that burns within you! May you say yes to victory! Yes to prosperity! Yes to deliverance! Yes to a better life! And yes to God! Amen.

Chapter 8 Reflection Questions

- What has been the most inspirational/impactful moment in your life?

- What could you share from your life that you think would be a great inspiration to someone else?

- What is your source of strength when you are faced with really difficult moments?

THE RIGHT STEP

If I can mask my feelings then no one will ever know
I can keep it to myself, no sign will I ever show
I can't let anyone know about the pain inside
So I tuck my tail and I run somewhere to hide
But no good reward comes to those who retreat
In spite of the mask your problems won't be obsolete
Free yourself and have no bounds from head to feet
Because no chain remains except those that one seeks to keep
Don't hide the identity that is meant to be revealed
Don't lose your blessing due to an identity concealed
I find that liberation is quite appealing
Because in liberation there is healing
In liberation there is kneeling
In liberation there is feeling
A feeling of triumph, a feeling of joy
A feeling that the man is no longer a boy
A feeling of love, we shout it to the world
A feeling that the woman is no longer a girl
I believe in you and your victory awaits
Believe me my friend this is the right step to take

By: Kendrick Savage

9

OUTSIDE SMILING/ INSIDE HURTING

> Never underestimate the pain of a person,
> because in all honesty, everyone is struggling.
> Some people are better at hiding it than others
>
> – Will Smith, American Actor

If we were to be honest Halloween comes many times a year for a lot of us. **A few steps in the right direction!** No, we are not dressed as ghost and goblins while parading through our neighborhoods, while hearing the words "trick or treat." But wearing a mask is more of a trick than a treat, you silly rabbit! Some of us trick ourselves into believing that we don't need anyone. Some of us believe that we are alone and can find ourselves on the verge of a total meltdown. Sometimes we wear the prettiest smiles and can carry the most polite conversations. Some of us are about to lose our minds, throw in the towel or even fall over the edge. You feel that you can't let anyone know about your struggles. You know you need prayer, support, and love. What will people think if you tell them, right? What will happen if they know you are not always as strong as you look? What if they knew you were scared about what's around the corner? When I was in high school, I had a friend that would always say, "Ken, I can't be doing that, I have an image to maintain!" LOL. We would laugh about that phrase all the time. The truth? That's exactly how a lot of us feel and the reason we feel like we have to present this perfect person to the world. Now, I'm not telling you to tell everyone your business. I just think we are all more alike than different. The problem is that most of us just hide it. Even those of us in church. We are still too afraid to just be honest and tell God, "look this is really how I feel and how I'm doing". Believe it or not, it will help liberate you and others if we were more motivated to share our similarities – our concerns, fears, weakness...**A few steps in the right direction!** Stop wearing this so call mask, attempting to hide how you really feel on the inside. Come out of this self-imprisonment. This feeling of imprisonment because of your job position, social position, or even your position in the church. If I have your attention, then go ahead take off your mask! I'll wait!

I know there are some people out there who you would be better off not confiding in – I get it! But if you need someone, then pray for God to send someone you can talk to. It doesn't have to be someone offering therapy, it could just be a friend that has experienced the same thing. God does love you and above all please seek Him first. Scripture says, **But seek ye first the kingdom of God, and his righteousness; and all these things shall be added unto you.**[1] What I am encouraging is for you to tell God how you really feel. Let him know your fears, your passions, how you need to be strengthened. Let him know how you want to be loved, how you want to be a better man or woman. This is your intervention and God is asking you will you take down your mask and talk to me, tell me where you hurt, tell me what you want in life. **A few steps in the right direction!** I am encouraging you to tell God, here I am Lord and I lay my problems at your feet, please don't pass me by. God I love you, God I need you, please don't pass me by!! Lord you know how I been fronting just trying to get by, please don't pass me by!! Call on the Lord, last time I checked you won't get a busy signal; He won't put you on hold and He won't hang the phone up in your face. You have nothing to lose my friend except your mask.

- A FEW STEPS IN THE RIGHT DIRECTION -

Who cares what other people will think? It is your life and you that needs the help. Truth be told, we all do. We all need somebody. We all need somebody to listen. Remember, this is about you, not them. **A few steps in the right direction!** I encourage you to do what you need in order for you to be healthy. I want you to get back to a place where you feel you can be productive. I want you to wear a smile that's not a part of a mask but one that is expressed by your true feelings. Actor, activist, and musician Tyler Merritt says, "the only way forward is not to hide ourselves, but to be as truthful as possible. About our lives. About what hurts. About who we are." A mask is made so that you can cover up what you don't want others to see physically most of the time. If you think about it when you are feeling vulnerable, weak, and full of emotion these can lead to some of the most revealing times. They are revealing because you find yourself in a place where it does not bother you whether someone knows or not. I have always believed that this shows strength more than it does weakness. I will tell you that the longer you mask your feelings and keep it all in you most definitely will make your situation even more difficult. The bible says, **And he said unto me, My grace is sufficient for thee: for my strength is made perfect in weakness.**[2]

It is when you are weak that you really are strong! He's your big brother! He's your source of strength and power. This is one Halloween party that I encourage you to leave and on your way out throw your mask in the garbage! **A few steps in the right direction!** My friend I encourage you to open up and let it out. I know that you want to shed the pounds; I want you to get rid of the weight that is holding you down emotionally, spiritually, and in all other possible ways. You were meant to be you. I titled this chapter as Outside Smiling/Inside Hurting because a lot of times we smile on the outside while trying to avoid the hurt on the inside. God wants you to open up to Him about everything you could possibly imagine. He wants to help you through your situation. You don't have to carry your burdens alone. **A few steps in the right direction!**

I know that sometimes wearing a mask seems as if it's a great thing to do. It keeps people believing you're at the top of your game.

Everyone is in belief that you're in control and you know just what you are doing. But it doesn't really matter what everybody else thinks! Especially when it is you that is hurting! God cares so much about how you may be feeling on the inside. Remember, you did not come out of the womb wearing a mask so why start now? I encourage you to live life strong, live life positive, and live life openly expressing to God the many thoughts and feelings that are on the inside of you. Many of our comic super heroes are heroes behind a mask. Well, you can become a super hero when you lose yours. **A few steps in the right direction!**

Chapter 9 Reflection Questions

- Do you feel like you are wearing a mask? Why?

- If you are wearing a mask, then do you think it is hurting anyone? Do you think it is hurting you?

- Is there anyone you feel you can let your mask down in front of? Why?

- In what ways can you be more honest with how you are feeling?

LIKE AN EAGLE

So many times, life's trials attempt to leave me blind.
I'm constantly wandering the forest trying to
climb the tallest trees while on bending knees.
First generation educated and through the
soul of my ancestors emancipated.
My adversaries, enemies, opponents,
challengers that is, have one job.
And that job is to break my will,
but what they don't understand is that you can't break a man
who was meant to be kept together,
purposed to be more than better,
and like eagles, I rise in stormy weather.
I've been given a voice and better still a choice to rise
with the sun and scorch the opposition.
And like the star that I am, I'll hang in position.
Shining because I've been polished and not
demolished, and viewed to set the mood.
And if that wasn't enough, I'm just getting started.
And you best to bet on me running my lane so successfully.
I admit that I will not quit.
My race is far from over.
My goal is to finish this race.
So, I keep a steady beat with my feet
and I run my race with a strong pace.
My eyes are focused and covered by grace
because I'm the man who understands he was meant to
be kept together, purposed to be more than better,
and like eagles, I will rise in stormy weather.

By: Kendrick Savage

10

THE GOLIATHS OF LIFE

> I guess it comes down to a simple choice,
> really. Get busy living or get busy dying
>
> – Andy Dufresne (from the movie - Shawshank Redemption)

I titled this chapter The Goliaths of Life because we all have faced some Goliaths. Let me explain by using the biblical story of David and Goliath. I love this story. First, I love how Goliath misjudges David. In the story, Goliath focuses on the appearance of David. He focuses on his youth and his occupation. To Goliath, David was no more than a young shepherd boy! The thought of David defeating Goliath seemed impossible, to Goliath. **A few steps in the right direction!** David's secret ingredient? His faith! Goliaths size didn't matter, Goliaths confidence didn't matter. All that talk Goliath was doing didn't matter. It is the perfect example for how we should face our own problems. Second, the thing that I like most about David in this situation is that he used what he had! **A few steps in the right direction!** I can't tell you how many times I have seen someone give up because they don't believe they are enough! They don't recognize the power in using what they have! How do you know if you have what you need? Trust me, you do! Your journey will always provide the preparation! Your journey has given you wisdom, strength, knowledge, and understanding. You just need to tap into it! **A few steps in the right direction!** Scripture reads, **Well done, thou good and faithful servant: thou hast been faithful over a few things, I will make thee ruler over many things: enter thou into the joy of thy lord.**[1] The third thing I loved about David was that he was able to focus on what being a servant had taught him. Again, you are enough, if only you pay attention to what you have already been blessed with. **A few steps in the right direction!** Some of us, when wondering if we are enough, go down a list that includes our job, our titles, and what society says we are and if that list doesn't provide the confidence we need, then we sometimes don't believe we can accomplish the impossible. But you are a lot more than a job, a nice house or car, or expensive wardrobe. Ultimately, those things fade. You see, David knew who he was, but most importantly, David knew whose he was and that made all the difference. David didn't reject his training, he accepted it, even though it wasn't as flamboyant as what others would think, it had provided all the training he needed to defeat Goliath. When David was doubted, he reminded them that he had taken care of his father's sheep and therefore he had learned how to fend off threats by protecting the sheep. What have you learned to fend off? What have you spent time protecting? What skills and tools have you learned from your previous triumphs? Whatever they are don't abandon them! They are still useful for your present situations! **A few steps in the right direction!**

The Goliath in your life may not be an eight foot tall giant. **A few steps in the right direction!** The Goliath in your life may be you speaking words of death on a day that the Lord has made. The Goliath in your life might be procrastination, anger, or childhood trauma. Whatever the situation is we all deal with giants. Some of us struggle with generational curses that we accept, gambling problems, academic problems we create for ourselves. What are you willing to do in order to defeat your Goliaths? Say it with me, "I can overcome my giants!" Don't let your Goliaths look at you and put a name on you. You don't ever accept defeat!

Perhaps you live in an environment that you do not feel is

conducive for success. Maybe there is violence, drugs, or verbal abuse. It may seem as if life has given you an unfair hand. You may feel like you have been born into a cycle that feels inescapable. These are all giants that can be overcome! I need you to believe! **A few steps in the right direction!** How did Muhammad Ali defeat the giant they called George Foreman? Well, besides the rope-a-dope, he believed he was even bigger! (If you are a youngsta, then you might need to look this up! OG's check in. I know ya'll know.) Muhammad Ali was not 8 feet tall but when he opened his mouth he could make you believe he was 10 foot tall. My point is, if you want to defeat your giants, then pray for what you need! **A few steps in the right direction!** I can only imagine that it was God that gave Ali the rope-a-dope tactic! God will give you a survival guide of how to defeat your giants. If you live in a drug infested neighborhood and you want a way out then pray for everything you need. You need shelter, protection, food, an education and somebody that is going to help you. A giant is no match for God. If you live in an environment of abuse, then I hope you pray for what you feel you need in order to overcome your situation. It just may be your prayer, determination, dedication, and relentless spirit that wrestles this giant to the ground where it belongs. You cannot give up on living life just because of what the situation looks like. You cannot give up on living life just because you're the only one that believes there is a better way! It does not matter what the problem looks like! I repeat it does not matter! If we base our survival on what the situation looks like, then many of us would have given up a long time ago. Focus on finding a solution! **A few steps in the right direction!** Solutions may look different for all of us and that's ok. The point is that you have to find what works and helps you. We cannot afford for you to give up! Trust me, giving up will cost you more than getting back up. So, if you happen to fall, then get back up, but whatever you do, just don't give up! **A few steps in the right direction!** Whether your giant is your professor, boss, money, health, food, parents, or siblings I expect you to keep marching toward victory! **A few steps in the right direction!**

    May you blaze a trail that will inspire others. You are a giant crusher! You get yourself together and know that this day, this day we declare victory for you! You will not and cannot be a victim of the giants around you. You are brilliant and you are brave. You are the victor and you will have victory and live victorious when you realize that everything you need in order to defeat the giants around you is one prayer away. Ask God to give you what you need in order to be the leader that will lead others out of Giantville just like God helped David. I pray God's blessings on your life. And just know that you can!

Chapter 10 Reflection Questions

- What are some Goliaths in your life?

- What are you doing or have done to overcome the Goliaths that you face?

- What would your life look life without these Goliaths?

A FRUSTRATED TALENT

Now what is it that makes a talent so vital like Americas next idol
Wear the badge of frustration like some title?
You see, the day before yesterday was the
day I almost through my life away
The day before yesterday was the day I couldn't find my way
And I was in a hole, in somewhat of a cave
If the walls had of collapsed it might have been my grave
Now you can measure this exterior that you think is superior
But sometimes this superior exterior feels quite inferior

These words might not be suited for
digestion its okay if you question
Because as of right now I'm wide open for suggestions
You see, sometimes its hurtful to a gentleman
Who feels that his personality is like quick sand
Like quicksand do my actions sink below the morning dew
And all the things I ever wanted I have no energy to pursue

Because the rules I made up for the game being played
Were the wrong rules and caused my goal to be delayed
And if I could remove my face I'd wring out all the tears
They would drop to the paper forming words that express my fears
Because its hard on a man that don't understand
How his next move feels like the wrong move, again quicksand

And no, I'm not elated but I'm quite frustrated
That my forward movement is being negated
And even though I was quite frustrated
I became concentrated that the next day
I had already made it

So even though
The day before yesterday I almost threw my life away
Those cave walls didn't collapse so I decided to stay
Because the day before yesterday was two days ago
And I'm still alive, the clothes have changed so
Two days after the day before yesterday is actually today
Which means I didn't throw my life away.

By: Kendrick Savage

11

WAKING UP WITH VICTORY

> I believe God had something more for me and I just kept working until He said, "Yes, now it's time."
>
> - Tabitha Brown, Actress and Author

Have you ever felt frustrated? I'm sure you have. That feeling that what you put out into the world is not coming back to you like it should. Or perhaps it's the feeling of nobody is trying but you. That is what the poem that introduces this chapter is about. It's about feeling frustrated. It's about weight or sometimes pressure that can get the best of us. However, it seems as if the rules being used are the wrong rules because the goal continues to slip away. Perhaps you feel like the work that you are doing for your family, your boss, yourself, friends and love ones totally goes unnoticed! There are no accolades and pats on the back. Have you ever felt like that? You have talent, dreams, and motivation but you are still bothered. It happens. Let's dive into this more.

You are blessed and you know it. God has blessed you to be a gem in your own light. You might even say you are a diamond. But truth be told, you are still frustrated! Is it because the dream seems like it will never come? Is it because you feel no one notices? How about we take a look into both.

What becomes more important to us in life? Is it the pats on the back? Is it recognition from multiple sources? Is it all the good things people say about us? Major recognition for all the so call good deeds we do? What if you never receive those things? Would you still continue to do what you are doing? Scripture says, **And let us not be weary in well doing: for in due season we shall reap, if we faint not.**[1] I'm with you, life can be so frustrating sometimes! Oh, and there's the other thing – life is not fair! It can be easy to allow these frustrations to get the best of you. Life can cause us to shift onto a detour of destruction simply because things are delayed and not denied. My encouragement to you is to always remember the following:

- Remember your WHY – WHY you chose to do something.
- Remember, what would happen if you gave up?
- Remember, you have been chosen for your opportunities.
- Remember, you are more seen and appreciated than you'll ever know.
    - People won't always tell you!
- Remember, stop worrying about results!

Let me take some time on the last bullet point. We are often so worried about results. You know, "the what happens after I do this?" Will people congratulate me? Will I be a big thing? This is why I say, "Remember why you are doing what you are doing" because that is what matters. If you get stuck on results, then it can paralyze you or even cause you to start doing things for the wrong reasons. **A few steps in the right direction!**

Now, let's transition to the person who is frustrated because it seems like the dream will never happen. I'm a big believer that God can meet you right where you are and not where you thought you were supposed to be. I am reminded of some lyrics by rap artist Jay-Z, "I'm in the hall already, on the wall already, I'm a work of art, I'm a Warhol already." **A few steps in the right direction!** I like those lyrics because I like the mentality. They also remind me of one of my earlier points – these lyrics represent results! So many of us are frustrated because we imagine ourselves as "something already" and I'm not saying you shouldn't visualize your success. You should! I am saying, make sure you separate the confidence boosters from the work it takes to get there. What's my point? You will get there! But it is going to take some time. Remember focus on the work, not the results! Follow me – Let's talk about victory!

My sophomore year in college I can recall waking up and not feeling victorious. It was the furthest thing from my mind. When I awoke I immediately was thinking about everything else – all of my frustrations or the things that were causing my frustrations! It took me some time but eventually I would replace those frustrations with more thoughts of victory! I stopped just reading about victory and listening to people talk about it and I started utilizing it in my own life! **A few steps in the right direction!** I started appreciating the fact that I was alive! I really gave thought to the fact that I had a new day to improve my life! I was victorious not because everything was perfect but because regardless of what life threw at me, I could always get up if I got knocked down. What anchored my belief? It was scriptures like this one: **These things I have spoken unto you, that in me ye might have peace. In the world ye shall have tribulation: but be of good cheer; I have overcome the world.**[2] I knew through prayer I had the victory. I knew God would see me through! And no matter what people said or believed about me, privately I had my own beliefs and source of confidence! I also held on to quotes like this one, "It is not the fall that counts, it is the rise after the fall that matters most." **A few steps in the right direction!** Everybody is going to fall, but we don't always choose to get back up! Those that do are normally a success.

I wasn't perfect – let's get that straight! I still had tough days and moments. But I got better at wrestling any thought or action of negativity to the ground and holding it there until it tapped out. **A few steps in the right direction!** Perhaps you do not share the same beliefs and values that I do. That is ok. I don't expect everyone to be the same. The advice still applies – you still have the victory! Just look around. There is always something to rejoice or be thankful for. If you so desire it, then there is no obstacle that will break you! No mountain will overshadow you! And no valley will be low enough to scare you from getting to the other side.

Victory will require many things. One being courage – be courageous enough to believe in yourself. May you also exercise your faith, trust, strength, and an unmovable, unshakeable bad to the bone attitude. What choice will you make today? **A few steps in the right direction!** Everything that you need in order to have a great day will first start with your choice of attitude about that successful, great, loving, adventuresome, and obstacle climbing day that God has blessed you with – it won't always be easy but it doesn't mean it's not meant for you. It is up to you to carry victory with you out the front door. You should keep victory in your car; keep it on your desk at work, at meetings on the job, and most importantly in your heart. Remember, as the captain you can either steer your course in a direction of doom or you can sail into the sunset of love, joy, peace, and the ability to overcome your obstacles. Victory awaits! Will you choose victory? Will you choose to overcome frustration? **A few steps in the right direction!**

Chapter 11 Reflection Questions

- What do you find yourself frustrated about the most?

- How do you typically respond to frustration? Write down some healthy ways you believe are great ways to handle frustration?

SPECIAL MESSAGE

BE A MENTOR

Mentors are special, they are special to life
We benefit from the wisdom they hold
As the stories unfold
They make the difference in the journey
Something like God's grace and mercy
Just to hear their voice enlightens the spirit
Inspiration is activated as soon as you hear it
They are special because of what they do
Showing care and concern for me and enough love for you
They are golden! They are precious souls!
Sometimes young! Sometimes old!
Every kid needs someone to love and someone to trust
Someone to help light the way, it's simply a must
A journey is rarely ever smooth
And It can sometimes be dark
You may need a helping hand, you may need a new spark
Mentors spark ideas, mentors invoke inspiration
Mentors create change, mentors change the nation
So, grab a hand and change a life
Create the change, make the sacrifice
Because you've been chosen
To help someone else be great
You've been chosen
To make their pathway straight

By: Kendrick Savage

S.H.A.P.E

SHOWING
HONOR
AND
PURPOSE
EVERYDAY

Relationships are ultimately what matter – our relationships with God and with other people. The key to becoming a mentor leader is learning how to put other people first. You see, the question that burns in the heart of the mentor leader is simply this: *What can I do to make other people better, to make them all that God created them to be?*

– Tony Dungy

Maya Angelou once said, "I come as one, but I stand as 10,000." I have not progressed on my journey alone. Though every time I stand to change a life, and I'm the only one seen, it is with deep gratitude that I know my 10,000 are with me! **A few steps in the right direction!** One of the greatest gifts that I have ever received in my life was having a mentor. It was someone that took time to listen to what I was going through and cared enough to help me past my stumbling blocks. It is truly something that has made all the difference. I cannot stress enough the importance of mentors. No one makes it alone, we all need someone. And if you are in position to mentor someone else, then think about it! We all have to reach back. You don't have to know everything and you don't have to have this squeaky clean journey! If that was the case, then no one would be a mentor. Being a mentor is about putting your neck on the line and doing whatever it takes to be there for someone else. I say, "putting your neck on the line" because you will get asked things you don't know, admit things you wished you hadn't of done, and discuss things you might be embarrassed about. Furthermore, it means teaching one about the ups and the downs of your life. It means saying no I don't know all the answers, but I can share my experiences with you. Most importantly, just be you! **A few steps in the right direction!**

I encourage you to not get to a place of complacency! That place where you either forget about others or too comfortable to help someone else. That place where you say, "Well I made to the top and that's all that matters." That place! If you think like that you have made it nowhere. I remind myself this very day that there is no good in achieving great success and never helping anyone else. You are not the only one that wants a better life. You are not the only one that wants to be a great father, husband, brother, co-worker, friend, or student. Let's do the best we can by reaching out and back the best that we can. Do your best to help change a life. Skip your favorite show for an hour and help a child in need. It just may be that hour that turns their life around. Skip a night out with the girls or the boys to mentor someone who is in desperate need of direction. Trust me one day you will look up and be glad you did. What could possibly be gained from it? Let's take a look:

- When I found people that took special interest in me, it made me feel like I had to make it! I just had too!
- I thought to myself if I make this decision I might hurt them so I better make a better decision.
- I thought to myself that I may not see all the greatness God has placed within me right now but I'm going to keep pushing to find out.

Those are just a few benefits. I enjoyed the day I knew that I was going to meet with my mentor. It is a special bond that no one could take away and it is a much needed bond. Remember mentors, no one is asking you to have all the answers. I hope that after reading this book you will be encouraged enough to live your own life with victory and that you will reach out to someone else who you know needs you. Someone that may be headed down the road that you were once headed down – whether good or bad, you can still provide direction. As a result of this I would like to talk to you about **S.H.A.P.E.**

This stands for SHOWING HONOR AND PURPOSE EVERYDAY. As a mentor the impact that most of us have in a person's life is that we help shape them. We help shape them by giving of our experiences and lessons that we have learned. We help shape them by showing them a better way if we know it. We also help shape them by showing them the love that they are due. Now, another way to help shape those that we mentor is by showing them honor and purpose every day. We can show them honor by having great respect for ourselves as well as for them. Teach them that respect for self is key for someone to respect them. Teach them that having respect for themselves means respecting the way they dress, talk, and handle themselves in all situations. Show them this by practicing it in your own life. Guess what? You won't be perfect at this! None of us are! **A few steps in the right direction!** If we want to help shape someone then show them that honor by exemplifying respect. Secondly, we can help shape those we mentor by showing them purpose every day. Let them know that it's not an accident that God allowed them to cross your path. It's not an accident that they were blessed to achieve success, get that great job, be a great husband, or great wife, mother, father, or friend.

We, also have to let them know that it is purpose that they finish what God blessed them to start. Some will want to walk away, and some will want to give up their dreams. But purpose is success and there is no giving up in purpose because purpose does not quit. Remember, if you want to mentor then what S.H.A.P.E will you give to those who need you. They are and will be watching you. Please take **a few steps in the right direction** with me and make a difference.

Former president, Barack Obama, once said, "What's better for us? Do we settle for the world as it is or do we work for the world as it should be?"

Whatever your answer is to this question, I pray that the words from this book have invigorated you and given you the confidence to use your gifts to make the world a better place!

I LOVE YOU!

NOTES

Introduction

1 Proverbs 4:7

Chapter 2: CAN EYE SEE?

1 Proverbs 29:18
2 Jeremiah 29:11
3 Matthew 5:14
4 John 10:10

Chapter 3: STEPS

1 Proverbs 3: 5 – 6
2 Matthew 6:26

Chapter 5: SHOES WITH SOUL

1 Romans 8:18
2 John 16:33
3 Proverbs 14:23
4 Job 13:15
5 Romans 12:12

Chapter 6: MORE THAN A SHELL

1 Romans 2:11
2 Luke 6:38
3 John 3:16

Chapter 7: RED CARPET

1   John 4:4

Chapter 8: THE TESTIMONY

1   Joshua 1:9
2   Isaiah 40:29-31

Chapter 9: OUTSIDE SMILING/INSIDE HURTING

1   Matthew 6:33
2   2 Corinthians 12:9

Chapter 10: THE GOLIATHS OF LIFE

1   Matthew 25:23

Chapter 11: WAKING UP WITH VICTORY

1   Galatians 6:9
2   John 16:33

ACKNOWLEGEMENTS

First and foremost, I want to thank God for placing this book on my heart to write during a difficult time years ago. You really helped me to write myself into victory! I also want to thank God for pushing me to give myself a chance!

Secondly, I have to thank my Amen corner – My wife Jamye, my oldest daughter Kurrie, my middle daughter Kenley, and my youngest daughter Kambry. Thank you for always being there for me and being the constant reminder of what's really important in life.

I want to thank my sister Monica and brother Melvin. Thank you for all the fun moments and having my back all these years! It's hard out here as a middle child LOL!

To all of my family back home in Oxford, MS – I love you all! Big thanks to all of the teachers that had an impact on me! Lafayette County Stand Up!!

Big thanks to my Ronald McNair brother – Dr. James Stewart! Thank you for reading my book, offering editing details, and supporting this project! Appreciate you bro!

I know better than to start naming people for this part – So, I just want to say to all of my friends, mentors, and supporters thank you so much! You know who you are. And to anyone out there that has ever helped me, offered me an opportunity, encouraged me, or just said a kind word, thank you! There are so many of you!

All the different church families I have visited and been a part of throughout the years, thank you!

A special thank you to my church family back home in Oxford, MS – Philadelphia M.B. Church. Thank you for providing such an awesome foundation and support system for me. I will forever be thankful of all the relationships, love, and support that has continued to follow me as I have ventured out to continue to make a difference! I am forever grateful!

CPSIA information can be obtained
at www.ICGtesting.com
Printed in the USA
BVHW031821140423
662386BV00018B/152